YELLOW ELEPHANT

Small and plastic, You kept it in your purse.
A tiny little elephant.
We always used to ask you to show it to us,
Do you still have your small, yellow companion?

It was very exciting to see,
For no other elephant is quite so tiny,
Or yellow, or plastic.
But fascinating just the same to us
As the elephants of the wild, or in the zoo.

Enclosed with shiny coins and crumpled notes,
Keeping them safe from harm.
It's bright yellowness kept happy
I've always wondered where he came from
Did you ever tell me?

I hope to see you soon, and ask you politely,
If I could maybe say "hello"
To your tiny, yellow elephant,
That used to live inside of your purse.

WITH LITTLE YOU: AT THE BEACH

The waves were flowing towards the shells in the sand,
Sunk by your feet, the child's spade,
'Mix sand with ocean water'
The brimmed tear of accomplishment.
Triumph as the mighty castle erupts,
Tumbling over your small feet
Sing over the child's cry, comforting.
The waves were giving water, fresh to build again.
Midday approaches
We splatter sun cream over ourselves
Spilling over the red beach towel
Rub it in so you don't get into trouble!
You laugh, strong as the Sun's heat
Summer with little you is rewarding.
Time to go home... my least favourite time of all.
Struggling to your feet, I hold you close,
'Mix sand with ocean water'
The glistening eye of Remembrance.
Pleased as your masterpiece stands,
Shadowing the foot-printed sand
Sing to the soft radio, calming.
The waves disappeared, promising to come back.

THE ZIP WIRE

Staring up and along, tentatively watching the brave young
boy perch them self up and onto a small tyre seat, you sweat
silently. Attached to a long metal chain, like giant paper clips;
hanging onto nothing but a long, thin wire that wobbles and
twangs. Trembling lips, you notice their feet as they push off,
and let go from the metal ramp. Nothing was going to stop
them.
Inspired, you feel ready. Beckoning your friend to push you
fiercely along the zip wire, you tell them to hold nothing back.
You want to be remembered as the bravest one that day.
Adrenaline is booted-up, into your system. Your 'natural',
Computer-conscience shuts down, and the sense of Play
installs within your bloodstream.
Holding tightly onto the chain, casually seeing if you can fit
your finger through the gaps of the links, you are taken by
surprise, swiftly swaying freely. Like forgetting you pressed
Start on your favourite video game, feeling lost and left
behind. Suddenly you feel the full-swing emotion as your
mind catches up with your body.
You feel the very last moments of your feet touching the last
part of the ramp, but you cannot reach the soft, damp bark
chips that the big-kids churned up on the turn before.
Your life flashes before your eyes, but you have no regrets.
However your default setting kicks in; yelling at your friend
pushing you, begging them to let you zoom free. You become
engulfed in the experience, overwhelmed.
You blink heavily, but the Virus inside of you unleashes the
power cable of vision for the last time. Pixelated blue sky,
getting closer yet further away, as you rock in mid-air,
bouncing against the large tractor-tyre locked onto the end of
the wire.
Within seconds it's all over. You're no longer scared of the
monstrous zip wire. The crowd of kids cheer at the sheer
beauty of the scene. At ease, you wave at them with one hand,
waiting for your friend to rush over to you, and help you off of
the sweaty tyre-seat. You exit the game, proud.

THE SWING SET

The least intimidating of the playground collection: a tall, majestic swing set.

Most children have a metal and rope swing set in their back garden. Where the grass invites them to land softly, against their blunt blades, that cushion their fall from the sky. Grass will later be mowed into lumpy-mash, just soft enough for a child to bare.

Learning how to swing is like getting one fish to follow your finger along the tank's glass. It is a challenge of the mind.

A child will never forget the day they fall off their swing. Knocking them harshly on the back of their head, the child is torn. No cry so severe; it burns the mother's heart to hear them so troubled, shocked and hurt.

Over time, cobwebs grow. Children will argue that Spiders are stopping them from playing on the swings. Even gullible parents know of the secret grudge: the swings have a one-up on their child.

Arriving at the park, the swings are sure to grab any child's attention.

Wooden, rusted, squeaky swings are most common. Who can get the highest, and least irritated of the awful noise, on the swings?

Children do not fear the tall, wobbling structure of the old swing set, badly cemented underground. They fear the wasps, attracted in the summer heat.

Wasps are the extreme terror of the mind. Children brave knowing they are attracted to the tall wooden structures, and moistened bark chips on the ground.   They avoid wasp's powerful stings all day long.

Standing steady on the swing, they test out their new-found skill. Excited to see how difficult it would be, to sustain comfort in standing tall, and swinging high.

THE RIVER OF LOVING YOU

We should have practiced our goodbyes
Like reciting the sheets of delicate music
That were left and forgotten by the campfire.
I could see the tears brimming in your eyes,
They made me never want to say goodbye.
So we just sat there.
The light wandered away, warning us:
Time was passing, and we were not prepared.

You rode on home in pain that night,
If I could, I would have written you out:
A song so strong that sails you back to me
But my gift is useless.
My poetry made you blush a fantastic smile,
One that held for over ten thousand seconds
Time was passing, but your smile did not quake.

When missing you became unbearable,
I would write you a new love song,
Reminding you that in my heart, we still loved
To dance together, in the middle of the ocean.
If I fell asleep beside you,
You would rock me awake softly,
Like the boathouse on the river on a stormy morning.

We didn't need the Sun to light the way forwards:
To show us that we were fixed together.
But we needed the Sun to remind us,
Life has a lot of winding rivers,
And it's easy to fall into the opposing current.
Only when falling down the steaming waterfall,
Did I realise how much I needed you,
To make me feel unassailable.
There was no rocking-motion to calm me.
Time crumbled slowly, so I could hear every heartbeat,
Every counting 'tick' and 'tock' of the glass metronome,

Shattering murderously, as my heart fell to pieces,
Reaching the steaming ocean before me,
And for a short, sharp moment, I heard you calling.

I needed bottles of answers stored in my heart,
To recognize how I felt for you.
I never felt confident with my own decisions:
The music I would write and send ashore,
Trapped in a cork-screw bottle,
Sent to the very depths of the profusion,
Taught me how to determine my path towards you.

I thought I didn't have the time, to play the music
That you wrote for me, while I slept in your arms
That tempestuous night.
I wish I had tried, my regrets heavier than any mistake
Anyone could've made before. But,
I hope you know I've been keeping your lyrics safe,
In the River of Loving You.

CAR RIDE HOME

Gasp for air,
The sudden awakening,
Like a child's nightmare.
Everything is heavy,
Can't you feel my heart,
Beating out, right in front of you?
Turning the stiff handle clockwise,
Embrace the wind as the window unwinds,
Stuffy air escapes and is renewed.
Gently accepting the white cold,
Greeting my face, calm,
I feel safe.
Resting my head gently on your shoulder,
Nested peacefully in your loving nature,
Put your arm around me, hold me closer.
Large gusts of Wind are heard,
But only gentle breezes touch,
My freckled skin.

LEMONS IN A BOWL

In year three I painted a bowl of fruit.
Focusing on the shapes involved,
How the composition lies,
Why the lemons in the bowl ~
are heavier than the thick paint,
I was lacquering onto the canvas paper.
Hours of tummy~turning anger,
Lemons; bright and yellow as fire,
My destructive talent, I hated my canvas.
Presentation evening:
I scavenge the hall quickly,
Wanting to find my painting,
It's hanging boldly on the board.
With my friends' golden paintings,
I point at all of theirs',
Diverting each parent's attention.
Anxiously wondering who notices
The painted bowl of lemons, grouped sour.
We bring the painting back home,
Exhausted I sleep, relieved it's over.
The bowl of lemons haunts my dreams.
The next morning, I travel the house,
Irritated, I notice the bowl of lemons,
Staring down at me,
From above the giant door frame.
I could never reach it,
Stuck above the door, for anyone to see.
The painting had won,
Against the perfection~minded
Eight~year~old artist.

MORNINGS WITH A CAT NAMED PONYO

I open my door in the morning,
To the green shining eyes and purring sounds
Of my cat. Rushing into my heart;
Winding between my ankles,
Meowing away what she dreamt last night,
All for me. Kind head rubs, wandering
Towards my bed to be lifted for a cuddle,
But I want to go the other way.

I give in. Carrying her like a baby,
Cradled in my soft arms,
She sneezes, almost every time.
The motion of big unruly steps for a cat
Her size, although impressively long,
She is very short.

Interrupting me, I spill soya milk everywhere,
Cheeky companion. Licking up what was spilt
I praise her with some biscuits
Carefully getting to my room again,
She follows. "Let me eat! Go eat!"
She pounces up and into my lap
Seconds later she head butts the bowl
From out of my hand, into my face.
When will I learn?

Stroking her to rest, she settles
After I finally finished eating.
Closed eyes, but she's not sleeping.
Patiently waiting for me to leave
I best reside here, before she wakes all over again.

CAT Vs. FLIES

Young Ponyo jumps curiously
Without an inch of stealth.
Focused, unfocused, focused once more,
A blue bottle is her prey.

Minutes turn into hours,
The search continues.
Paw-only swipes through mid-air,
Wobbling on her two back legs,
She thumps the blue bottle softly
Against the skirting board,
Squashed, under the carpet.

The blue bottle is to never be seen again
But still buzzes when Ponyo stomps
Over the carpet,
Under her favourite windowsill.

She refuses to be a cat at times
Stung by a wasp on her front paw
Digestion was her revenge
Pulling a funny face,
Meowing at her mother,
"I ate the wasp that attacked me!"
Proud with confusion.

Her inquisitive little mind
Not questioning her actions,
Set off into the garden again,
To see what she could find.

THE LOVE I WANTED TO KEEP

Lips softer than an Angel's heart,
Eyes that glow in the Sun's reflection
Ripple in the ocean,
You smile a light
That shines right through my reality.
Focus strongly as you hold my chin upwards.
The perfect angle; kissed by the ultimate,
Devil in disguise

The once-so-warm heart turned cold.
Apologies shouldn't tear these trees apart;
They took so long to intertwine
Their branches like
Our small fingers interlocking,
A promise without words.
Perfect clasp,
Hopeful for a summer full of bliss
With you that would have been possible
But now our energy is escaping.

Can't you see this is salvageable?
We have everything in common,
Yet, no spiced feelings shared
Why did you change your mind?
Late nights,
Hours of conversation, turned to dust:
Compliments burnt in the pure white fire,
Singed to ashes,
Nothing will make sense between us again.

Your eyes glistening as my tears are held back,
With the reigns held by the tamer's,
Hands fragile like the petals of the flowers,
Stinging nettles sharp,
But so many bees were inside of those beautiful flowers.
Graceful was you watching over the bees

But keeping an eye on me, I saw,
Protected in your comforting branches
Never have I experienced such welcoming vulnerability

I thought you cared
Gestures genuine to my heart
Passionate actions to my skin
Willing, as I trembled over the roots of our trees,
That was once content being under the soil.
I want to stay tightly tangled with you,
But against the World and my reality
I had to escape this toxicity that remained
Still left suffering

Our branches that was once so strong,
Rotting away from each other
Grasping, begging for newfound oxygen
Our roots have been destroyed

NIGHTMARES

Sleeping alone is terrifying.
I hold on to the very last star,
I see at night,
Until my mind drifts to sleep.

Tucked in tightly;
I hope the warmth of four blankets,
Ignites the warmth I feel from you,
But it just makes me restless.

Clutching the edges of my pillows,
Shuffling the sheets from over me,
I suffer ferocious heat
Calling the demons to torment.

Nightmare after nightmare,
There's no time to calm down.
Surely I'm too old for this?
I give up on sleeping.

The constant being-chased,
Hiding from the monsters,
That only I know to be people.
Why am I so scared of them?

I am still weak and vulnerable,
I cannot uncover myself with bravery.
Every child finds their own sanctuary,
When protected in blankets and sheets.

PLAYING WITH MY FUTURE

I mostly remember the days when it used to rain,
When I would be stuck in the house, alone
With the purple cube, a retro video-games console.
Setting up, untangling all the wires from yesterday,
I scan my collection of games, what do I want to play?
I never completed one game.

I've always grown up, imagining to have a successful life:
To be likeable, have a million-and-one jobs,
And to have a lot of loving pets.

But, like the videogames, I fear more as I get older.
The people I meet are mean and working,
Only to pay the higher-people.
There's very little chance for me,
To succeed. To complete just one of these videogames,
At an Amateur level, 16XP and with 0 gold rings,
Is more than I am capable of... but I accept this challenge.

FRIENDS COME AND GO

Friends are the people you care for and trust
Every day, normal people wandering the Earth,
Just like you and me.
But we build connections with many people,
Depending on certain qualities, we notice;
How they walk, talk, pose,
What their attitude is,
Who they hang around with,
When they're happy or sad...
A first impression is a big, old test,
To sell yourself to the category 'Popular'.

We are taught "never judge a book by its cover"
But we are all victims of evaluating each other.
These people have feelings.
Some even have a mind of their own;
Thoughts conflicting with who they are-
And who you thought they were.
But together, you learn to support them.

Friendship groups usually circulate through schools
But I moved several times as a child.
Losing contact with my very best of friends
Never have I had a better collection of memories,
Than trying out karate on the school field,
Getting covered head to toe in mud, daily.
Standing on the backs of their BMX's, then
Climbing trees and sitting by the water
Hiding in the farmer's field of tall wheat.

Weeks, months, maybe even years will pass,
Holding their hand until the day
The turtledoves die, without so much
Of a warning; terminating our life together,
The train has reached its final destination.

And we all have to leave and look around
This new, exciting area, meeting new people.

But memories still exist:
The first trust-exercises,
Going to the park,
Swimming in the ocean.
These things you did, will be yours.
A scrapbook of the mind,
Pages torn and scribbled over,
We all have some arguments.
But lots of alternating coloured pages,
Your favourite, then theirs.
You practice writing in their flare,
So it doesn't look like something you made alone.

A recorded video that stops in places,
Rewinds to replay ten times at once;
All for the sake of seeing their smile.
But it's worth it.
Some parts may be in black and white,
And noticeably more colourful in others.
Other parts may be too difficult to handle
So you sit with a tissue, hugging the pillow
They got you that first Christmas,
When all they knew was you liked taking naps.
This mind-forged montage of your Friendship,
Is to be protected forever.

PRO-FOOTBALLING EXPERIENCE

Summer was the only time we could go onto the school field.
Muddy children ran wild, as if they'd run away from the Sun,
Glorious and hot, they dared to look right into it for fun.
Play Leaders couldn't control carefree infants
Rolling in the small sand pit like funny elephants.
But I wanted to play football.

Rounding up the stragglers of the shade,
Convincing them we would, one day, be the best
Footballers of Stambridge, there was no time to rest,
As autumn was fast-approaching...

Setting up the pitch, aligning coloured cones,
Together we had a team of four:
A goalie, defender, the one in the middle, and me.
We charged and kicked our hearts out!
But couldn't control our very own feet.
We fell one by one, sun-stained in the heat.

LONE FLAMINGO

Why do I stand on one foot?
I am not an Ostrich,
Nor do I bury my head into the sand
For when I am scared,
I stand on one foot.

Searching for a fellow white bird,
Loneliness has left me bleached.
I desire to be inked,
Pink, or yellow, like my beak
I take a glimpse at another,
Fantastically painted, I call her
But I stand on one foot.

Tall, I stretch up to the greenery
An orange, as alone as I
I found use for my elevated leg,
To bury this orange.
This is why, I stand on one foot.

FIZZY DRINKS

I'm six years old.
The camera is rolling,
It's not my birthday,
It's not Christmas, or Easter,
Why am I getting so much attention?

I sit back, and try to understand
How to embrace myself,
For a beaker of Fizzy Drink.
Everyone enjoys it, right,
So what's the big deal?

Exploding fireworks!
My taste buds cry,
Surprised, it spills.
Shockingly cool,
My skin tingles.

Ten years on,
Sat by myself
Smiling as the glass fills
In my control,
Addicted to Fizzy Drinks.

Spitting out of the glass
Taste twangs against my tongue
Pulling a funny face,
My first Fizzy Drink memory
Rewind the tape to start all over again

SCARED OF THE DARK

We all have fears growing up in this world.
I am scared of many things.
I am not afraid to admit this,
For stubborn doors have to be forced open,
From time to time, to clean the dust.

I am petrified of the dark.
Being alone, in a big empty space...
When the light goes out,
And the only way for me to see anything,
Is to trust myself, that I am safe.

Mirrors get turned over,
Terrified to look into them,
Like seeing myself in the window –
When darkness rules this hemisphere,
My heart jumps out from my body,
Adrenaline flushing through, severe.

Looking around my room in awe,
Everything seems to be in order...
Nothing to trip me over~
To break any bones in my body;
Not that I ever have broken a bone before.
I take one brave step, after another...

But after just a moment of having no light,
Visuals become vivid. Weird things that don't exist suddenly
do.
It's clear to me that I am not alone.
I cannot see feasible things now,
When the light goes out, I blur, stunned.

Shadows are invented;
From the gaps between the curtains,

The glass above my bedroom door,
I shouldn't have this feeling~
That I'm being watched.
Approaching my curtain stiff, to check...

I just can't handle this anymore!
I give in! I give up! Call it a day,
Where I can't go to sleep in the dark,
Like everybody else!
So I keep my light turned on.

Only some nights do I brave to sleep,
In the incompetent darkness.
And in the corner of my eye I focus~
So hard, I practically invent this Ghost,
Babysitting me, silent.
I actually attempt talking to it sometimes.

It's not supernatural,
It's clearly paranoia,
Of the heart that knows Spirits exist.
Have you ever woken up at 3am,
Feeling pressure, pushed against your heart?
It happens and it hurts. Are you scared?

New~found heavy breathing, and headaches
Lasting a lifetime, every night.
How does my heart keep up?
Relapsing the same programme;
Terror of the dark,
That visits me every night.

CHEMICAL TRAILS

Why are there such streaks;
White and bulky, polluting
The natural blue sky?
Only Aeroplanes could soar,
Leaving trails of expanding colour.

They are not clouds,
Not natural,
Not fluffy like candyfloss,
Nor are they sugar coated.
But we sugar coat them.

Clouds should be round,
Like little puffs of sheep bodies
Clustered within the atmosphere.
Daydreaming children count,
These sheep should send to sleep.

But Chemical trails within the sky
Fall heavily, like acid rain.
But not obvious as the rare rainfall,
Like carbon monoxide, silently killing,
The daydreaming innocent.

CATFISH

Rivalry of the Big and Small,
Catfish should be friends.
Small. hiding all the time,
The Coral was its mother.
Big Catfish swims,
Attacking viciously;
Eating tails of other fish,
It was an evil one.
But the protecting Coral,
Who had worn weak,
Could not stand any longer.
Small Catfish was left,
To defend for itself...

The other fish swam,
Flicked their tails in the stones,
Barricading the Small Catfish
Safe, but Big Catfish was tough

Demolishing the wall,
With one swoosh of his tail,
The stones and sand caved in,
And Small Catfish was gone.

MEMORIES LAST FOREVER

I found myself screaming "STAY!"
Even though you left hours ago.
I'm sat by the fire, finally out of cans
And broken glass bottles~
That was once full of answers.

Sometimes I think too much,
Overpowering times you would speak to me.
I faded out into the background noise,
Perishing in the flames of knowledge~
You knew I had not been listening.

It was not my choice, my plan,
Controlling my free thoughts, steady;
Stop for just a moment, pains me to my core.
Because I really wanted to hear your voice,
Staring into your soul, I ignored the words.

Why is it so hard to concentrate?
On listening to your side of the conversation?
It's not just you who I struggle listening to.
It's rare for me to talk myself into new~
Situations full of hope, are they waiting?

You know I'm going to be here,
Until my thoughts unite in tranquillity.
Meditating dawn 'til dusk,
The challenge is to silence my mind
To heal itself at last.

Please! I can hook my heart~
To your long~vacant smile
That was once so warm, inviting.
On the countdown to breaking~point
We asked too many "why's" and not "when's".

I regret not taking more photos,
And scrapbooking every funny thing
You've said to me this year
Because they say memories last forever~
That way.

WHERE DO I GO FROM HERE?

One being, wishing upon a star
Wishing you knew who you are
Waves crash against your walls
That were built behind the calls
For you when you fell behind
The society you should now find
Try to fit in they say,
Why cant you have it your way?
You wonder as you continued
Your journey to be renewed
Renounced, reclaimed as a person
Your heart may be weighed by a ton
But know you always have me here
Supportive, caring, I'm here to cheer.

WALKING AROUND THE CORNER

Walking with your head held high,
Shoulders back, and looking half-assertive.
Everyone watches, as you pass on by,
But inside you are shattering into a pieces.
Keeping your eyes focused in front of you,
The subtle-sweat streams down your face.
Breathing heavily, panic rages the taboo-
In question: Is this normal?

Swinging around the corner,
You wonder; Did the indicating car, imagine
Me walking out- into its road?
Did the driver even notice, as the engine-
Drove down the road, I kept to the path of?
Relieved, I realize, I will never know;
Them or how they saw the situation.
Adrenaline will continue to show
Through my body, as I speed-up, in anticipation.

POWER OF SPEECH

Controlling beyond imagination:
Words have so much power,
They should not be capable of.
Holding hands with their creator,
Destroying emotions, as if happiness
Was made to crumble;
As soon as the child looks up at the Sun,
With a sparkling heart and soul,
They cry out in sudden agony.
Naïve to the realisation;
What they love is what killed them,
And they will continue to fall in love
With words they are yet to hear.

THE WANDERER

Wild and free, an unknown cat
Wanders the field of buttercups
Soundly sleeping in the bushes,
She awoken in the mist of my shadow.
Silhouette; she ponders her first impression
Questioning my aura, she looks up
Bright blue eyes, sparkling vastly
I squat down on the grass,
Hand held out to her just metres away
Wandering around me, I stay still
Quiet and smiling, peaceful in her company
I allow her to follow her nose kindly.
Rolling her scent into the grass,
She allows me to pet her behind the ears,
And feel her fur, stripy and soft.

MINEFIELD

Trapped. In this metaphorical minefield,
Where only poetry makes any sense.
Twisting and turning like a child
Desperate to awake from a nightmare.
There's very little hope that I will wake,
Surrounded by suffocating darkness,
I swallow all of my words and reach out
For I have nothing else to lose.
Walking through this black hole,
With sweating palms held out, open
I'm sure to catch all the pain and misery
Invented by the underworld's Lord,
But with hope still strong,
I endeavour to grip onto any kindness,
A white feather, of my guardian,
A star, rainbow or strike of lightning,
As long as it helps me feel something,
Anything other than this cold air,
Like a demon breathing down my neck.
I will not stop until I find the mine of Chance,
That may be in my way.

A VEGAN IN THE FAMILY

It's always been Me growing up differently,
Forming another kind of branch on the family tree.
Instead of a pretty flower or root,
I'm the branch who grows all the fruit.
My own individuality, seems to affect all,
As if not eating meat causes a brawl.

We share and we chat, we laugh and we play,
But nobody else seems to feel the same way,
About the way poor animals are harmed,
Living their precious little lives: battery farmed.
Hoping deep down, I am helping them out,
My older sister goes to vigils to shout-
To get involved with animal rights,
Keeping their hearts loving and bright.

THE PEOPLE YOU NEED IN YOUR LIFE

Who thinks outside of the box?
Ready to answer the unimaginable,
Before the possibility of such questions~
Even being invented, has arrived?
Those who sit and stare, patiently~
Watching, waiting to share their
Valuable and sentimental information~
With the world, make the Future clear.
Eyes look upwards in their bright clarity,
Always brimming with passionate colours.
Like petrol-fuelled tears: highly explosive,
Shining in the direction of their dreams.
They open up only to a select few,
Similar to the rarest of all the flower buds,
Seeking for the perfect, bravest bees
To collect their pollen.
These are the people~
You need in your life.

FLYING STARFISH

Every day, I complete ordinary Sea-Star activities.
Sticking to the stones in the sand,
Absorbing vital nutrients day by day.
But the water is changing…
The sea is filling with dark energy,
Sharp and broken 'things' appear-
Without warning.
Routines are not made to be broken
But today I need to make a change…

Shuffling over my rocky bed,
I let the water wash me ashore,
Fleeing from my home, I regret my choice.
Instantly the sense of danger arises.
Under attack! I have been captured…
Taken into flight, in the gullet of a bird.
Petrified I fight to fall back into the ocean,
I pray to return to my rocky bed.

Thrown and bitten, I scream in terror
"I am not a fish!" I cry, "I am not your prey!"
Unheard, I get tossed and carried away,
Never to be seen again, on the beach of Nairn.

HEDGEHOG ADVENTURES

Awakening in my pile of Autumn leaves,
I yawn with happiness, stretching my legs,
I stick my nose out of the leaves and sniff!
It's evening. The air is subtle and musky…
I feel safe to take my first steps outside.
After a long, warm sleep, I've been prepared~
To endure in my nightly, 1~mile stroll.

Setting off, into the golden, glowing Sunset,
I look up and study the scenery in awe,
Lots of flashing lights, illuminating the sky,
To the shallow, sleek star~struck field of nature.
I wish I could move my leaf~pile house here!
The steady silence is easy to fall in love with:
You can wander with no anxiety, simply existing.

An abundance of berries blinds me~
With joy! I munch on their fruitful colours.
Regaining energy, I come across something new;
A small hut, covered in leaves, it's cosy~looking.
I look inside to see if it's a vacant little house,
Feeling like the naughty, young 'Goldilocks'.
Eventually, I begin to forget what was important,
My small pile of leaves, the perfect Hedgehog Home.

I, THE HAMSTER

Thousands of tiny, inaudible sounds,
Pierce through the skin in an instant.
It's hard to cope with such small ears,
Noises that should be tiny, have huge effect.
Child scraping against the metal bars
As the sun rises, irritates, And
I just want to sleep and block it all out.

A radio: Instruments and Vocals too strong for lungs to bare.
They should've exploded by now,
Jingles and slogans, child-happy laughter that seems
otherwise amusing,
Increases the pain in my head…
But I know I am loved.

Called out for, I wrinkle my nose, as the sawdust-nest cascades
around me.
Bright light almost blinds and there's a potent pong,
of soapy hands reaching out for my fragile body…
A cuddle! So comforting and warm,
Releasing all anger from the sounds I suffer.

SLEEPING IS A FORM OF ART

Sleeping is the most creative form of art!
Merging the reality of life,
Into the realm of fantasy.
Where would you rather be?
Going to work, or dancing in the Sun?
Walking to a shop, or exploring a jungle?
These things we could do in real life…
But who takes the time,
To feel the passion of nature?
In dreams, no heat is too suffocating,
No Sun will ever burn, no pain is ever felt.
Swimming in the oceans in a dream,
A fearless experience!
The interesting facts of the world,
Rules Define qualities of every individual,
Are beyond escapable. Freedom lies within a Dream.
Take chances and doze off in the Summer's Sun.
Or return to the reality of life, dreaming of it.

MYSTICAL PALACE

Have you ever experienced self-peace?
The accomplished feeling of floating-
Out of your body, but you remain calm?
Surrounding yourself with the quiet Auras;
Charming Spirits will guide you there,
To a Mystical Palace for you to call Home.
As you are removed from a bustling reality,
Levitate your soul and harmonise your Spirit
To the melody played by the shining scales,
And splashing tails of Koi fish in the pond.

WEAKER THAN THE WIND

Sometimes the wind blows so hard,
It's difficult to feel if you're still there~
Beside me, hidden by gushes of all forces,
Attacking from all angles against us.
Forwards, is supposedly the best way to go,
But backwards, I know what to look out for,
A sure-fire way to happiness, and innocence,
Back to a time when I was intrigued to be little.

How different my life could have been,
Plays my mind harsher than a broken record.
The wind suffocates all possible confidence,
It squeezes my hand so tightly; I cannot trust it.
As if fate has something out to get me,
To throw me so far down the ladder of self-esteem.
I've struggled to climb for many years now,
Just to reach the vision of you, my strong future-self.
I'm wobbling ferociously but I've never held on~
With such passion. Hoping to prove to this cruel world,
That I am stronger than it believes.

YOUR VOICE CAN CURE THIS WASTELAND

Sitting pretty; a perfect creation.
Looking up and out of the window,
Travelling at Super-Speed, you turn,
Studying the view as city merges to stone,
Fields blend with Wasteland, surrounding
Your beating heart, you remain still, for
You cannot change this world.

Trapped air fills your lungs heavily,
As if falling through the sky in peace-
Is normal. You are not allowed to fight,
Or whine, or repeat words that sound,
Like honest screams found deep from your soul.
Pulling on the strings of your voice's harp,
Only beautiful melodies were heard.
Because "Nothing is wrong with Planet Earth".

IMPORTANCE OF MONEY

Money does not grow on trees,
Ducks have abnormal knees.
Money is a state-of-the-art,
Potatoes will never fart.
Coins are made from metal and gold,
While Homeless feet are left so cold.
Notes with Royal faces printed in ink,
How many have been dropped down the sink?
Money is something we do not need,
Only for the rich, to strive with greed.

EXPLORE YOUR SPIRITUALITY

Truly explore your mind for just a moment…
Sit in solitude and respect the air around you,
Do you feel fulfilment within yourself?
Is being Proud an oxymoron,
When you are dying inside with crippling anxiety?

Hear the whispers carried through the wind.
Study the water droplets that fall,
Flowing from the ends of your hair in the shower,
Calming motion of hundreds of water beads,
Free-falling in synchronized spirals.

Bathe in nature's beauty.
Surround yourself with the essence-
Of the sanctuary, known as the Wild.
Listen to the soft chirping of the birds,
Feel the emotion trembling from the sky.

As the Sun falls gracefully to the West,
Calling the non-luminous Moon,
From behind the clouds, to watch over us.
Stars whizz around the darkening sky,
I wonder if they really just are… 'Stars'.

Supernovas occur rapid, screaming,
Into the depths of a black hole.
Illuminating its galaxy, steadily bouncing near,
But we stand open-minded, reluctantly,
Clear Skies open before us, supporting our needs.

Waiting to feel more open-minded,
Teasing my mind with sleep. Cosy,
Resting against the pillows,
Tense muscles retract at last,
Allowing my Chakras to measure my content state.

Positivity rushes through me,
Like false-honesty, scared of the truth.
Burning lips and tainted eyes,
Everyone thinks that I'm doing fine,
Little do they know, it's a cruel, harsh world.

FLOWERS GROWING IN HARMONY

Why do flowers grow,
On fragmented soil,
Churned and nitrated?
Flowers so confident,
Anyone can see their beauty,
From fresh, green stems~
Arising from seedlings,
Dropped by the birds,
Wind~buried deep;
Unhealthy and toxic,
Composted in desolate land.

How do flowers grow,
Tall and wise, when
Embedded into the soil,
Of No~Man's Land?
Rebelling against –
Humanity's destruction,
Symbolising peace, restoration.
Representing a new start,
Blossoming, with a new~leaf.
We may not know How,
But the Flowers teach us Why.

THE SHORT GIFRAFFE RESCUE

Sheltered from the rain I stand
Short, like no other.
Discontented in wilderness of white,
Fur or Skin, I cannot tell,
But I am the only one, who is blank.
A canvas, you may say.
Preparing for burst of energetic sprays,
of Lightning-fuelled ink to come.
There is no way for me to tell,
What the future holds for me.

You found me, warm and graceful
Like no other, you look like a kangaroo
of the modern age.
You introduce yourself as a man,
Someone who understands what it's like
To not be coloured-in.
If we were in a story book,
We would remain, black and white.
Although I cannot say, you have a defined outline,
In a black marker pen.
But features that would need to be made apparent.

Welcoming me into your home,
it's roomy and I do not feel short.
I waddle on through,
The slippery floor is unnatural, why is it here?
Submerge your feet into grass and mud.
Notice how my hooves clip and clop,
Like that of a noble steed.
But I am not a horse.

You comfort me well, with chips and BBQ sauce.
Is this how you survive?
Potatoes are a product of the Earth,
I applaud your innocence.

But I would rather feast upon the small apple tree,
The luscious plant from behind your house.

I enjoy the new flavours of golden-ripe fruit,
That cannot be found in the wild.
Some good has come out of this Modern Age.
Before long I feel an incredible sensation.
The art of happiness has made me blossom.
Spurts of colour, appearing in splashes over my stumpy-body.
The mouth-watering essence lingers,
As my legs tingle, my canvas is no longer blank.

For I am bronzing faintly under the summer's Sun,
Dark intriguing spots and rough patches bloom,
Like the bud of a flower,
Opening up for the whole World to see.
Finally I am similar to the others.
I have fur, or coloured skin,
But it doesn't matter which.
I feel fuzzy and warm inside,
And it's all thanks to you.

Hoping to receive the best-of-both worlds,
I invite you to come along with me.
Grow short, stumpy apple trees for me,
And I promise I'll share with the taller Giraffes.
I would love for you to stay with me,
But for now, I ask for you to come back soon.

I MISS THE POND

I miss the Pond,
How fresh the water used to be,
Fish would swim freely.
Frogs hopped on the intertwined lily pads,
Playing games with the buzzy-bees.
Glorious watercress would sprout,
And stun honourably, flowers pink and gold.
Clusters of bulrushes protecting us,
Guarding the water's edge,
From the Bench where Monsters reside.

From time to time, there would be Noise.
Harrowing vibrations, rippling in the water,
Disrupting our natural routine,
Swimming in circles,
This was nonsense.
Inconsiderate, evil nature,
Why have you allowed them here?
We cannot fight them.
Suffering, we tell them to leave,
But they bribe us with "bread".

Monsters with a substance so enticing,
But one by one, Ducks fell ill,
They laughed and smiled,
Gathering in troublesome groups:
Feeding in abundance,
We cannot waste what they give us.
We shouldn't eat what they throw at us.
I feel guilty, for not warning the others.
I suffer alone, in this Pond.

Cold, dark nights, ducks fear of death...
Who could've thought, with such innocence:
The cutest of the Pond's inhabitants,
We are terrified of the unknown.

I miss the Pond,
When there was no such thing
As Monsters, or Rubbish, or Litter
When we could glide like swans,
On the other side of the beavers' dam.
We shiver and quake with broad quacks,
Mistaken for being happy, we are not.
We want sanctuary in our Pond.

BEHIND A POEM IS ANOTHER POEM

Should all poems really rhyme?
Should they use words like sublime?
What techniques really make a poem;
The ones where you tell a story,
Of where you've been goin'?

Children find poems fun at first,
But taught to wear 'em out in a burst
Of a balloon-red simile or metaphor
What are these techniques needed for?

They do not create the reality
They create visuals of similarity
So everyone can have their own poem
That relates to where they've been goin'.

MY FAVOURITE ANIMAL IS A DOLPHIN

Grey with speckled silver,
Washing them all over.
Watching in their trance,
Glittery dolphins dance.

In spotlight white and bold,
With shining scales so cold.
Only fish who prank, are
Caught by ol' man, Hank.

No one expected the lobster,
To be cooked up by a monster.
As it was known as a friend,
Of the pub just 'round the bend.

Sea-lions balance on balls,
and eat fish up on their stalls.
It's funny they eat them raw,
When we cook them up before.

Some people will protect,
The Dolphins of neglect.
As they are just like people,
Who don't have to visit a steeple.

GIRL'S VIEW ON 'FORMULA 1'

Almost everyone is intrigued by speed.
But why are Go-Karts so fascinating?
No speed limits, No guarantee of protection,
We all love the risking thrill of danger.

Superstar go-carters in hi-tech cars,
That look Like little rocket ships with wheels
Race competitively in interesting cities.
Azerbaijan, who knew it even existed?

Can they even see the track very well?
With helmets so large and round.
Barely seeing over the nose of their rocket,
Surely this is madness!

Go-getter racers expected to win,
Crash reluctantly into barriers, in fire.
Members of the crowd may leave,
Disheartened, but faith still strong.

What is a Safety Car?
Does it take them safely home?
It travels around the track,
And disappears without a trace .

Would you watch to see the race,
Or to find out how it's made?
Not the cars, but camera angles;
How they follow and watch racers.

LIFE OF AN OTTER

I wake up every morning, happy to see you,
Holding your hand, floating on the water.
Peaceful motion, submerged in placidity,
There's no rushing to reach our destination.
We allow the water to take care of us,
Our fur fuzzy, noses wet,
The life of an Otter is sweet.

We are not fans of eating prey;
Survival is easier than this.
We find tall, fruitful bulrushes,
And scavenge for nuts to graze upon,
We live hand in hand with the fish.
They help propel us upstream,
The life of an Otter is honest.

Gracefully arriving, we feast our eyes:
The enchanting swamp of kelp,
A glossy, seaweed canopy over
The water's surface, enticing us in.
A deep-sea treatment, rewarding us,
Watching you dive in, I absorb my new reality.
Life of an Otter is fulfilling.

Printed in Great Britain
by Amazon